M000110506

ISBN: 978-1-7358613-1-9 (ebook)
ISBN: 978-1-7358613-0-2 (paperback)

Front cover image by Laura Matteson.
Book design by Laura Matteson.

First printing edition 2020.

www.EssentialsWithAmy.com

Dear Caregiver,

Between court dates, visits, therapy appointments, and general chaos, if someone had recommended one more thing, I might have thrown something. Foster Care and Adoption are the best hardest thing we ever did. I knew I needed more help and less stress but had nowhere to look. I needed accessible and simplified resources. I needed someone to tell me to do steps 1,2,3, and please, no more than 3! We had oils in our house. On a good day, I might drop some Peace and Calming on the kids and use a mix of lavender and coconut oil for diaper changes, but honestly, that was all the capacity I had.

I didn't have time for classes and lots of research. Most of my research was parenting and trauma-related. I got stuck after our second adoption. One kiddo wasn't sleeping, and one needed a sensory-rich day. I was tired, yelling, and wanting to escape. I committed to 30 days of using Frankincense (literally a swipe across my forehead) and a couple of drops of Progessence Plus (a hormone supporting oil). I felt like a different woman at the end of those 30 days. I was yelling less and much more content. I knew these were the tools we needed for less stressed parents, calmer kids, and better connections.

This book has been in my heart for four years. I wanted something simple for moms (and dads) to use. This resource would encompass both essential oils and connections. My heart is for moms to feel more content so they can connect. My heart is for kids to feel empowered to feel their emotions and have tools they can use, too.

As they say on the airplane, put the oxygen on yourself first, so the next section is just for you. Parent Care goes through some simple self-care tips, easy to use daily planner, and a couple of recipes.

My hope is this book is encouraging and empowering to you and your family.

Much Love

-Amy

PS Wayne, J & B, love you more!

2

Table of Contents

FDA DISCLAIMER:

Where's that Blend?

Simple Ways You Can Practice Self Care

Be Consistent With Routine

Use the My Scent-sational Day sheet on the next page to help you plan

Drink More Water!

I'm a better mom when I'm a hydrated mom

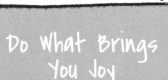

Find A "No Filter Friend"

Someone you can share all the ups and downs with, who is an encouragement to you

Do What Brings You Joy

Cooking, movement, podcasts, writing... Start with 5-10 mins a day

Draw An Epsom Salt Bath

These baths can help replenish your magnesium and soothe tired muscles. Here's a Soothing Soak recipe you can use:

SOOTHE SOAK

Find A Counselor

When I was at my lowest point, I did everything on this page and found a counselor. This quote is one of my favorites: "You cannot lead a child to a place of healing if you do not know the way yourself." - Dr. Karyn Purvis

Mix 2 Cups Epsom Salts + 2 Cups Baking Soda + 4 drops Lavender and 4 drops Raven - Add to a hot bath and relax.

**TIP: Use other oils of your choice, up the salt and baking soda to 4 cups and add a bottle of hydrogen peroxide to the bath for extra body system support.

Mix 10 drops of Frankincense, 10 drops of Lavender, and 10 drops of Stress Away into a 10ml roller, then top with a carrier oil.

TIP: This can be applied to wrists and chest as perfume.

My Scent-sational Day

Write down your favorite mixtures and oils from this book in the chart below to reference quickly and set up YOUR best oil routine.

MORNING	EVENING

MORNING	EVENING

MORNING	EVENING

Rolling Through Your Day —

Mid-morning & Daytime

Get Moving Roller Blend

10 drops Endoflex
5 drops Ylang Ylang or Joy
Mix in roller and apply to ankles
or neck of slow moving kiddo

Rootbeer Floats

4 Drops of Stress Away
2 Drops of Wintergreen

Tips for Mom
Reapply Endoflex and Calm Mom Blend. Super B and Ningxia Nitro are great
supplements for an afternoon energy boost.

School aged kiddos often need a boost
mid day. Here are list of options:

Nasal Inhaler: drop peppermint, stress away
or valor on a cotton wick. These are plastic and
easy to drop in a backpack.

Notes of Calm: 1 drop of Stress Away
on a note in their lunch or 1-2 drops
of Stress Away or Lavender
on their favorite lovie.

Wake up

Good Morning Diffuser Blend

3 drops Peppermint
3 drops Citrus Fresh

Sunshine Vitality Booster

1 ounce Ningxia Red
2 drops of Orange Vitality
can add to juice

— From Early Rise to Rest

Throughout The Day

DIFFUSER BLENDS

Smells Like Candy

3 Drops Stress Away
2 Drops Peppermint

**Homework Helper
Diffuser Blend**

3 drops Rosemary
3 drops Lemon
2 drops Peppermint

Focus Roller Blend

10 Drops Cedarwood
10 Drops Lavender
10 Drops Vetiver
Top with carrier oil,
apply to back of neck
by brain stem

If you have a little person who isn't in school,
a little dab of Peace & Calming on the ears can
be soothing during that 3-6 pm time frame.
Another favorite is the Tranquility Roll-On .

Night

Lavender and Cedarwood are best buddies
for bedtime. A few drops of each in the
diffuser or on the bottoms of your feet can
help your body drive off into a restful sleep.

Connection & Play

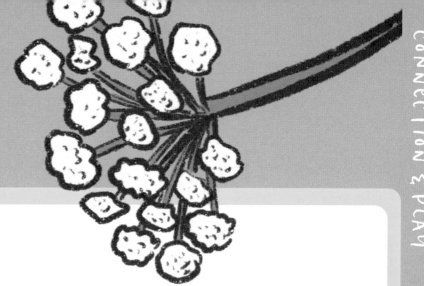

"Play disarms fear, builds connectedness, teaches social skills, and social competencies for life."
– Dr. Karyn Purvis

About a year into foster care we were introduced to a book called The Connected Child. It turned our parenting upside down. We pretty much shelved our learned parenting techniques. Counselors walked me through my own history and equipped us with connecting tools. Play being one of them.

One of my hopes is that this book will give you ways to play and connect with your children. This section is filled with some of my favorite nurturing activities for building trust and engaging in play.

Supplies:

1. Assorted bandages: (Band-Aids, Welly Bravery Badges, Dollar spot)
2. Shareable snack: gummies, chocolate chips, cut up fruit, crackers

Both activities will consist of giving and receiving care.

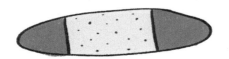

Inside Out Hurts

1. Grab bandages.
2. Grab Lavender, Owie, Stress Away & Valor.
3. Find a comfortable place to sit.
4. Ask if anyone has outside hurts.
5. Once a hurt has been identified, ask if you can apply a bandage.
6. Show them an outside hurt you have (may have to get creative if you don't have an actual one).
7. Let them put a bandage on you.
8. Ask if anyone has any inside hurts.
9. Adults usually start and share an inside hurt- example: "I was thinking about our dog who passed and was sad about that."
10. Then put a bandage on your shirt by your heart.
11. Ask kids if anyone has an inside hurt, let them talk about it and ask if you can put a bandage on their shirt. Lavender or Owie can be used on outside hurts. Stress Away or Valor can be applied to wrists for inside hurts.

This activity provides a simple way to talk about feelings and giving and receiving care. Giving and receiving are fundamental in building connection and trust.

Super Snack Attack
(can be done one-on-one or with the whole family)

1. Set up your diffuser with your kiddo's favorite blend.
2. Wash your hands.
3. Grab a shareable snack.
4. Find a comfortable place to sit.
5. Everyone gets 3-4 snacks in their hands.
6. You first ask your child if you can feed them a snack.
7. Wait for your child to respond "Yes."
8. Feed your child the snack.
9. Your child asks you if they can feed you a snack.
10. Your child waits for you to respond "Yes."
11. They feed you a snack.
12. Repeat until everyone has had a couple of turns.

We always chose special gummies for this activity. It allowed us to provide safety in a fun way, build trust and for them to learn to receive care and give care.

More Activities

If you are a new foster parent grab an oil like **Lavender or Stress Away** and wear it everyday. Diffuse it, put it on your little people's lovies, blankets, stuffed animals. This will eventually signal the brain that you are safe, you come when I call, this home is safe. Having a continuity of smell with comfort & care will create new patterns of connection and bonding. This can work for adoptive kids too.

Stuck/Motivation

Endoflex and Ylang Ylang mixed 2 parts Endoflex 1 part Ylang Ylang is our "Get Moving" blend. We use this in the morning or when one of our kids get "stuck" and has a hard time moving through a transition.

Scented Slime

Elmer's glitter glue
4-6 drops of favorite essential oil (Stress Away, Lavender, & Joy are fun choices)

1 Tsp Baking Soda
3 TBSP Contact lens solution
Airtight container
Plastic spoon for mixing

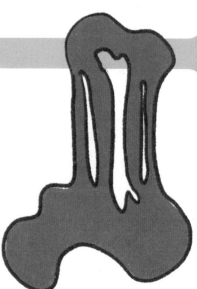

Pour glue into a glass mixing bowl.
Add baking soda and mix with a plastic spoon.
Slowly add contact lens solution one tablespoon at a time.
Continue mixing in the bowl until the glue has clumped together, isn't sticking to the bowl.
Add more contact solution until you have achieved the correct consistency.
Add essential oils and knead with your hands.
Store in an airtight container.

Play Dough

2 cups all purpose flour
1/2 cup salt
2 tablespoons cream of tartar
1.5 cups boiling water

2 tablespoons vegetable oil
10-12 drops essential oil (more or less may be needed depending on the oil you choose)
food coloring - optional

Mix the flour, salt, and cream of tarter together in a large bowl.
Combine your essential oil with the vegetable oil and mix into the dry ingredients.
Boil the water and add food coloring directly to water.
Pour 1 cup of your boiling water into the mixture and stir, adding the additional
1/2 cup of water slowly until it isn't sticky.
Knead for 3-5 minutes or until dough is smooth.

Sunshine Dough: add Citrus Fresh
Chill: add Valor or Peace & Calming
Play Away: add Stress Away

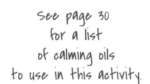 See page 30 for a list of calming oils to use in this activity.

Snow Balls Calming Activity

You will need:

3 calming oils   3 cotton balls

Place one drop on one cotton ball.
Have your child guess which cotton ball matches which oil. A fun game that gets them smelling calming oils.

The Welcome Sign

New places feel scary for all of us, until we feel like we belong there. One way to help your foster or adopted child feel welcome is by giving them a space of their own with their name on it. Names are personal and help make the new space feel comfortable. You can use the sign on the next page to create in a quiet place in your home.

For more activities visit: **www.EssentialsWithAmy.com/Resources**
and follow our facebook page.

13

Routine & sleep

Bedtime can be the hardest time as a parent and child. There tends to be heightened separation anxiety, more fear of the unknown, and uneasiness. Here's another time of day when consistency is key.

Here are a few tips for bedtime.

1. Set bedtime
2. A story or prayer time
3. Soothing music
4. A dim night light
5. A favorite stuffed animal or blanket
6. A soothing bath
7. Oil Application & Diffuser set-up
8. A drink of water
9. A protein rich snack
10. A sensory activity like a wheel barrel walk to bed

EVENING OIL /SUPPLEMENT ROUTINE

1. Pick a blend or single for each child
2. Pick an immunity supporting oil like Thieves
3. Set out any evening supplements: Mighty Pro, Super C Chewables, Mightyvites
4. Roll calming oils and blends around neck and ears
5. Roll immunity oils on spine or bottoms of feet

Oily sleep tips

OIL SPOTLIGHT:

Sleepyize is a blend of calming and quieting oils. It promotes an atmosphere conducive to a calm, restful sleep. Whether diffused or applied topically, Sleepyize is an excellent way to help you or your child naturally relax at the end of the day.

SUPER SLEEPER SINGLES

✳ ✳ ✳

Cedarwood
Frankincense
Lavender
Vetiver
Orange
Ylang Ylang

SUPER SLEEPER BLENDS

✳ ✳ ✳

Sleepyize
Peace & Calming
Tranquil Roll-on
Sacred Mountain
Stress Away
Rutavala
Valor
Seedlings Calm
White Angelica

SUPER SLEEPER SUPPLEMENTS

✳ ✳ ✳

Immupro*
Sleep Essence*
MegaCal
Mighty Probiotic

*THESE CONTAIN MELATONIN

MANGNESIUM CALCIUM DRINK

THE GOOD NIGHT BLEND

4 drops Lavender
2 drops Frankincense
2 drops Peace & Calming

MAKE A DIFFUSER BOMB

✳ ✳ ✳

A Diffuser Bomb is when you make your favorite diffuser blend in bulk. Take an empty dropper bottle and add your favorite blend to it.

Diffuser Bomb Recipe
1 dropper
30 drops Cedarwood
30 drops Lavender
Grab your dropper and hit all the bedroom diffusers without carrying ALL the bottles around the house. Simply drop 6 drops in each diffuser and add water.

Diffuser Bombs can done for any of your favorite blends. In the Spring, we love to mix up bulk Lemon Lavender and Peppermint.

Restful diffuser blends

Snoozy Spray

5 drops Lavender
3 drops Valor
3 drops Frankincense
pinch of salt or splash
of witch hazel
Top off with water

Mix and add to
a 2oz spray bottle
Spray on pillows,
sheets and blankets

Sweet Dreams
4 drops Frankincense
2 drops Sleepyize

Unwind
3 drops Peace & Calming
2 drops Lavender

Best Rest
3 drops Lavender
3 drops Cedarwood

Diffusing is a simple swap for candles and aerosol room sprays. They reduce synthetic fragrance and provide calming aromas for sleep. Diffusing is one way to lessen your home's toxin load.

Diffuser tips: Diffusers run for 4-6 hours and will turn off when they are empty. Most diffusers have light options and our new Feather the Owl diffuser has a night light and sound machine.

To clean, gently wipe the metal plate with a soft cloth.

Body Systems

Immunity & The Gut

Immunity and the Gut

More and more research is showing the link between our gut health and brain health. Often called the second brain, the gut is responsible for the majority of the body's production of serotonin. We know serotonin is a "feel good" hormone.

Pre & Probiotics are key to good gut bacteria. The best part of our new Kidscents Mightypro is it contains both a pre & probiotic. These are easy to take and tasty like a pixie stick minus the sugar kick. In our house, adults and kids both take this!

The gut is also key to good immune health.
This is a quote from an article from John Hopkins University:
"A huge proportion of your immune system is actually in your GI tract," says Dan Peterson, assistant professor of pathology at the Johns Hopkins University School of Medicine. "The immune system is inside your body, and the bacteria are outside your body. And yet they interact."

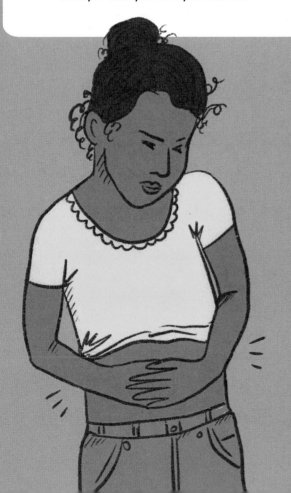

ROLLERS FOR HAPPY TUMMIES

Happy Tummy Roller

5 drops DiGize
5 drops Peppermint
5 drops Lemon
Top off with carrier oil

Tummy Magic

1 roller fitment
1 5 mL Tummygize
Add fitment to Tummygize & Voila! Roller ready!

Tummygize is already pre-diluted.

Whole Body Wellness

ACE's and Wellness

You've most likely heard of Adverse Childhood Experiences. These are experiences that researchers have shown affect long term mental and physical health. (For more information look a the work of Dr. Nadine Burke-Harris)

Because our children (and maybe even ourselves) have had these experiences, they tend to have compromised immune systems. We saw chronic colds, ear infections and suseptability to any common illness time and time again when we fostered.

We began swapping out synthetic laden laundry products, personal care products, air fresheners, and candles. We swapped many of these with the Thieves line of products, diffusers and DIY room sprays. Within months we saw an upswing in health & fewer missed days of school.

Thieves Roll On

A prediluted, roller top, all-in-one

Be Well Roller

20 drops Thieves
20 Frankincense
15 drops Lemon
5 drops Oregano (optional)
Add to a 10 ml roller
& top with carrier oil

Diffuser Blend

4 drops Purification
3 drops Lemon
3 drops Stress Away

Regulated Through The Seasons

WINTER WELLNESS

Thieves Tea
1 cup warm herbal or black tea
1 teaspoon raw honey
1-2 drops of Thieves Vitality
This is a perfect warm winter drink

Honey Drop
1 tsp of raw honey
1 drop Orange Vitality
1 drop Thieves Vitality
Place on spoon and
let disolve in mouth.
Soothing to the throat.

KEEP YOUR "BE WELL" ROLLER HANDY ALL WINTER (PG 25)

SUMMER SUPPORT

So Peachy Diffuser Blend
5 drops Orange
3 drops Valor
2 drops Cedarwood

Bug Off Roller
Mix 10 drops Lavender, 10 drops
Purification, 5 drops Peppermint
Top with carrier oil

Sunkissed Skin Soother
Fill a 1 cup container with 1 cup of
Aloe Gel, 10 drops Lavender, 5
drops Copaiba, 4 drops Peppermint
Mix and store in fridge.
Apply to sunkissed skin.

SPRING SCENTS

In Bloom
5 Lavender
5 Lemon
2 Peppermint

Breath Easy
5 drops Raven
5 drops Frankincense
5 drops Peppermint

Smelly Pop Supplies
1 popcicle stick
1 rubber band
1 cotton ball
1 3x3 square of fabric
2 drops of your
favorite oil

Instructions
1. Drop oils onto cotton ball.
2. Place cotton ball onto center of back side of fabric.
3. Place popcicle stick into the middle of the cotton ball and fold fabric around cotton ball and stick.

4. Secure rubber band around the base of the cotton ball.
Kids can carry their essential oil "lollipop" in the the car or backpack.

FALL FEELS

Comforts of Home
3 drops Rosemary
3 drops Clove
3 drops Orange

Crisp Leaves
3 drops Raven
3 drops Thieves

PERFECT SEASON TO START ROLLING ON THIEVES

DIFFUSER BLENDS

Bottled up Emotions

If this foster care/adoption journey isn't full of all the emotions I don't know what is. As a mom, I can easily have every emotion under the sun. Some days it's all of them: joy, anger, overwhelm, grief, exhaustion and delight. Some days it's just one.

For our kids, many times the emotions of grief, loss and confusion come out looking like anger and lack of obedience or attention.

The next page shows some of our favorite oils for emotions.

> On our "How To use Oils" page at the back of the book, you'll see a graphic of how smell affects the brain. There was a turning point in our oil journey when we discovered how trauma affects fight, flight and freeze and how oils go straight to the amygdala. We became intentional about oils and emotions. Oils are a fantastic tool when our emotions are stuck or overwhelmed.

Calm That Nervous System

White Angelica: This is going to become a favorite of yours if you tend to feel everyone else's emotions plus your own. I like to use this on my the wrists and shoulders. One of our kiddos takes on all the feelings and this leads to to heightened emotions. I add a drop of White Angelica to the crown of their head, and a drop of Clarity to base of their neck.

'Tude Tamer Roller:
10 ml roller
10 drops Lavender
10 drops Orange
Top off with carrier oil

Stress Away: It basically explains itself! It is an all seasons oil. I keep it in my car and will shake a few drops in the back seat right before I pick them up from school. We also have an Orb diffuser from Young Living we keep in the car.

Also, check out the Calm Mom Blend (pg 12)

Clarity and Frankincense: are a dynamic duo that can help clear the brain fog and help me focus.

Endoflex: Our whole family is a fan of Endoflex. Perfect for moody days and a great energizer. We apply to necks and ankles. This is a tween/teen must have!

Valor: We call this Bravery in a Bottle. Our son particularly likes this one. We call it his Brave Boy oil. We use this before doctor and dentist appointments and any new situations.

Cranky Days:
Our go-to is a drop of Purification on the forehead. It can also be combined with Lavender, Valor or Release.
Other options: Juvaflex and Joy.

Just for Kids

Young Living's topical and aromatic Kidscents products developed and diluted especially for children!

Owie™

Never leave home without it! This Kidscents essential blend is a soothing option for your child. Apply Owie™ topically to improve the appearance of your child's skin. Crash! Bam! Boom! Owie to the rescue!

SniffleEase™

SniffleEase™ is a rejuvenating and refreshing blend formulated just for kids. Add a roller fitment to SniffleEase and roll-on chest or feet for easy application when kids have the sniffles.

SleepyIze™

Apply SleepyIze™ to the back of the neck, feet, or wrists every night! Diffuse SleepyIze™ at bedtime for a peaceful aromatic environment.

Geneyus™

GeneYus™ is an excellent blend to diffuse for young minds that are focusing and concentrating on projects. We apply this on our kids before school. I particularly like to apply it at the base of the skull/neck area.

TummyGize™

TummyGize™ is a relaxing, quieting blend that can be applied directly on little tummies.

Other products in the Kidscents line include: Shampoo, Lotion, Bath Gel, Toothpaste, Probiotics, Multivitamins, and Enzymes.

The Starter Kit

Most people start their oil journey with the Premium Starter Kit. It has been perfectly designed with a diffuser and twelve everyday oils. This oil collection gives you oils that can be used for each section of this book. If you don't have oils yet, please visit **www.EssentialsWithAmy.com/GetStarted.** Here are few uses for each:

 **Thieves**: apply to soles of feet before school, day care or bed

 **Lemon:** a natural remedy for all things sticky

 **Peppermint:** Add to diffuser during homework or the afternoon slump

 **Lavender:** sprinkle on your favorite blanket for soothing sleep

 **Frankincense:** moms and dads swipe this across your forehead for a calming effect

 **DiGize:** apply to belly or drop under tongue for digestive support

 **Raven:** mix with a little coconut oil for a soothing chest rub

 **Panaway:** apply to muscles after exercise, sports or dance

 **Stress Away:** apply to wrists for calming, add to diffuser

 **Peace & Calming:** Mix with water and a pinch of salt for a calming room spray

 **Valor:** Bravery in a Bottle, apply behind ears for an extra boost of bravery/confidence

 **Citrus Fresh:** ditch the dryer sheets and instead add this oil to wool dryer balls

Make It Your Own

Try out each oil/blend from this book and as you find scents that help
you through certain emotions dab a drop of the oil below.
Fill in the name of the oil and it will be ready for you when you need it!

MY HAPPY BLEND:

MY MAD BLEND:

MY SCARED BLEND:

MY EXCITED BLEND:

MY SAD BLEND:

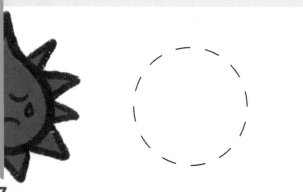

MY RESTLESS BLEND:

Make It Your Own

Like every good thing we do for ourselves and our kids, consistency is key. To simplify your oil routine create a space for your oils. Have them out where you can see them.

I love round tiered shelves, small cake stands, acrylic nail polish holders and small shelves. Discount stores often have a variety of options.

You can keep the process of making your own blends and rollers simple by having a few of these on hand:

Carrier Oil- for dilution and making roller bottles

Coconut oil- for quick muscle or chest rubs

Baking soda- for carpet refresher and soothing soak

Epsom salts- for aromatic soothing baths

Roller bottles- you can customize a roller for each member of the family

Spray bottles-for linen & room spray, and Thieves Cleaner

Our Favorite for:

_____
_____
_____
_____
_____
_____

Our Favorite for:

_____
_____
_____
_____
_____
_____

Our Favorite for:

_____
_____
_____
_____
_____
_____

Our Favorite for:

_____
_____
_____
_____
_____
_____

Directions: Cut out the cards above and fill them out with your favorite oils and blends for your children. Place them where you will need them most so you can find your favorite blends and oils quickly.

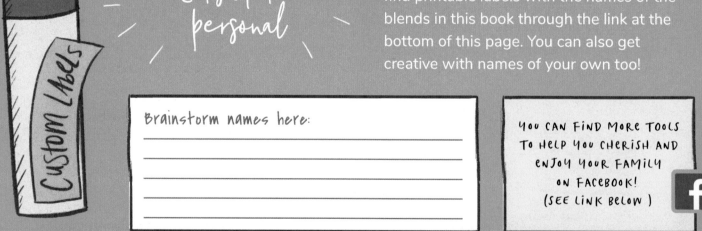

Let's Get personal

Custom Labels

A great way to personalize your oil blends is to add labels to the roller bottles. You can find printable labels with the names of the blends in this book through the link at the bottom of this page. You can also get creative with names of your own too!

Brainstorm names here:
_____
_____
_____
_____

YOU CAN FIND MORE TOOLS TO HELP YOU CHERISH AND ENJOY YOUR FAMILY ON FACEBOOK! (SEE LINK BELOW)

For printables & activities visit: **www.EssentialsWithAmy.com/Resources**

How to Use Oils

OIL TERMS

DIFFUSER: A tool that adds essential oils into your air

ROLLER BOTTLES: Jars with rollers in the cap to make it easier for you to roll oils onto your skin directly

OIL BLEND: A mix of different essential oils to get a blend of smells and effects

GEL CAPSULE: Cellulose coating for your oils so you can take them in a vitamin-like format for internal use.

VITALITY OILS: Young Living's Vitality line of oils are designed for internal use.

CARRIER OIL: These are oils used for diluting. We keep coconut oil in our kitchen. This makes it easy to whip up a chest rub or muscle rub quick, fast and in a hurry! Fractionated Coconut Oil, Young Living's V6 and sweet almond oil are great carriers as well.

COCONUT YL V-6 ALMOND OLIVE OR GRAPESEED

SAFETY TIPS

1. Start slow with a few drops and dilute as needed. (dilution recommended for children under 6)
2. Citrus oils are photosensitive. Avoid applying them topically and going into the sun.
3. Oils are not to be used in eyes or ears.
4. Should oils get in your eyes, apply carrier oil around eyes and wipes with a cloth.
5. Some oils are considered "hot" like Thieves, Peppermint and Oregano. If you notice skin redness, add carrier to skin.

TOPICAL

Pour a drop or two of oils in your hands and apply to the desired location. You can always add a drop of carrier oil to help dilute. Massage into the skin.

THE FEET ARE A PERFECT PLACE TO APPLY oils. They have large pores for quick absorption. Right before bed, I ask my kids to show me their feet. They kick up their feet and we apply their evening oils.

Roller Bottles are great to have on hand. You can pour 20 drops of oil or oil combination into to a 10 ml roller. Top off with the carrier oil of your choice, shake and apply.

INTERNAL

gel capsule

Add a few drops of any Vitality essential oil to a vegetable capsule, fill the rest with a carrier oil. We like olive oil for our capsules.

under tongue

Mild vitality oils can be placed under the tongue for quick absorbtion. We often use Digize under the tongue to support our digestive system.

for cooking

Our oils are potent. Go low and slow until you reach the flavor you are looking for. You can also dip a toothpick in the oil and then swirl into your recipes.

add to water

The whole line of Citrus Vitality oils make for a refreshing beverage. We have the new oil infused Vitality Water Drops, too.

AROMATIC

Inhaling essential oils allows the oils to directly affect the brain. You can see from the graphic below that your sense of smell directly affects the limbic system. The limbic system is the center of control for emotions, memories, mood, behavior and hunger/thirst cravings.

OLFACTORY SYSTEM

The aroma travels directly to the middle of the brain through the olfactory bulb. Then it makes it's way to the limbic system, where neurochemicals are released and processed. It then relaxs or stimulates depending on the essential oil that's used.*

NASAL CAVITY · OLFACTORY BULB · OLFACTORY NEURONS · LIMBIC SYSTEM of the BRAIN

INHALING

Place a drop of essential oil in your hand, then rub palms together and cup over the nose and mouth. I usually take 2-3 deep breaths and then apply the remainder to my shoulders, neck or belly.

DIFFUSING

Diffusing oils is the best way to create a mood in your home. Peppermint and Citrus Fresh are a great way to start the morning alert and refreshed. Lavender and Copaiba before bedtime will set the mood for sleep. We have diffusers in each room of our house filled with our favorite bedtime blends.

Each kiddo has one by their bedside. We use this in lieu of room sprays that are filled with synthetic frangrances.

34

My Favorite Parenting Resources

We love the book "**The Connected Child**" by Karyn B. Purvis, Ph.D, David R. Cross, Ph.D, and Wendy Lyons Sunshine, "**The Empowered Parent Podcast with Kayla and Ryan North**" hosted by Chris Turner and the "Empowered to Connect" website at **empoweredtoconnect.org**.

The Connected Parent: Real-Life Strategies for Building Trust and Attachment by Lisa Qualls and Dr. Karyn Purvis

There are also Parenting with Connection facebook groups, too.

These skills we have learned have helped us regulate ourselves and help co-regulate our kids.

OTHER RESOURCES

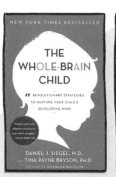
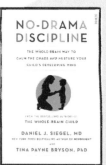

I also recommend the following books by Daniel J. Siegel, M.D. and Tina Payne Bryson, Ph.D.

"**The Whole-Brain Child**"

"**No-Drama Discipline**"

"**The YES Brain**"

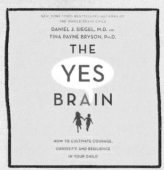